Your First
AQUARIUM

—— Sylvan Cohen, M.D. ——

Pages 2 and 3:
Pages 34 and 35:
Photos by B. Kahl.

t.f.h.

©1993
By T.F.H. Publications,
Inc., Neptune, N.J.
07753 USA

———— • ————

T.F.H. Publications,
The Spinney,
Parklands, Denmead,
Portsmouth
PO77AR
England

G000125886

Tank Size

In choosing an aquarium the general principle that must be followed is to match the aquarium to the size and number of fishes to be kept in it. Unfortunately, the beginner characteristically keeps adding fishes to his original setup at random, frequently without realizing the degree of crowding he is creating.

Overpopulating an aquarium is one of the most frequent causes of failure in the hobby. A number of factors account for this. The most obvious ones are a shortage of oxygen and the presence of excess carbon dioxide in the water. Under long-term crowded conditions excess nitrogenous compounds (ammonia, nitrates, and nitrites) also build up in the water and will have a debilitating effect on the fishes. Plants help to clear this excess nitrogen to a considerable extent, since they are able to utilize nitrates, the end product of the nitrogen cycle, but even the plants will suffer when the concentration becomes too great.

An additional factor is the transmission of diseases from one fish to another. Most significant fish diseases are infections of various types, and their spread in the aquarium can be extremely rapid under crowded conditions. The hobbyist must realize the remarkable difference between a small confined body of water such as an aquarium and the fish's natural situation in a lake, stream, or river. The confinement alone stresses the fishes, but crowded conditions make things much worse, often leading to a decrease in the vitality and eventually the health of the fishes.

There is no absolute rule to follow regarding the number of fishes that can be kept in an aquarium. A safe guide is to keep the number of fishes in a tank that can be maintained without requiring supplemental oxygenation or filtration. These aids to aquarium cleanliness and health are almost universally used, but the fish's lives preferably should not be placed in jeopardy if there happens to be an interruption in service, such as during power failures or failures of the pumps or filters. Filtration and aeration should be used to increase the safety factor and they help to maintain the overall healthiness of the tank and its inhabitants. It should not be supposed, though, that an aquarium should be pushed to the limit of its fish-holding capacity just because it's equipped with a filter. That's the kind of thing that can be done only by experts—and even for them it often turns out to be a bad gamble. As a beginner, you're better off avoiding anything that will cut down your margin for error, and crowding is one of them.

10- and 20-gallon aquaria

These are the usual sizes for community tanks. They are large enough for a variety of compatible fishes such as mixed livebearers or small characins. Approximately 10 to 20 fishes of the usual 1- to 2-inch size can be safely maintained. Beginners are most often successful with mixed livebearers and may find a special advantage in raising swordtails and platies. The hobbyist with excess healthy colorful fish may be pleasantly surprised to find that his local dealer will often be willing to take these fish in on trade for others or for supplies. Guppies are more difficult to dispose of profitably. Many new and colorful varieties of swordtails and platies are now available, including some very attractive high-finned strains.

Most characins, danios, and barbs will also do well in tanks of this size. Especially popular are neon and cardinal tetras, head-and-tail-lights, and zebras. Some of the barbs tend to be fin nippers, and this must be considered when mixing species.

This is also the smallest size tank suitable for medium-sized cichlids, but the individual fish temperament must be considered. Some cichlids are aggressive and bullies; others have a placid disposition with others of their own kind, especially if they are a mated pair. Initial spawning behavior can be rough, and torn fins are the rule rather than the exception. Angelfish, however, tend to be big bluffers and rarely do serious damage to fishes their own size.

Larger aquaria

Almost any variety of tropical fish available can be kept in these large tanks, but even here one must constantly guard against the tendency to overcrowd the aquarium. The experienced hobbyist recognizes the misconception that a crowded tank is attractive, and finds that fewer but more carefully chosen varieties are much more attractive than a helter-skelter mixture of a dozen species of fishes paying no attention to one another.

The shape of the aquarium depends on the purposes for which it is intended. Tall, narrow aquaria with a large front glass face are excellent for show, but will accommodate fewer fishes because of the limited surface area available for oxygen and carbon dioxide transfer. Flatter, shallower tanks are best for raising fry and young fish, since they have abundant air surface and swimming room. The standard size aquaria are good for general use. They are also cheaper than the odd shapes and sizes. Tall tanks are especially expensive because of the extra thick glass required to withstand the greater water pressure at the bottom.

Fish retailers will often provide various package deals on aquarium set-ups that conveniently include most of the important tank necessities. Photo by V. Serbin.

With a little decorative imagination your first aquarium can be converted into a fascinating living picture, making for an interesting addition to the home furnishings. Photo by B. Kahl.

Temperature

The usual advice given to beginning hobbyists is to maintain the temperature in tropical fish tanks at 75° to 78°F. Actually, many fishes will do well at somewhat cooler temperatures if these are attained slowly and can be maintained without further sudden drops. Larger bodies of water change temperature very slowly and can be kept at a steady state much more readily than smaller tanks. For the average home aquarium the 75° to 78°F range seems to work quite well.

Thermostat-heater combinations

The single unit thermostat-heater is probably the most popular heating device for aquariums. Heaters are available in both non-submersible and submersible types. The latter are more expensive but more easily hidden. They allow each tank to be individually controlled, depending on the variety of fishes to be maintained and the condition desired.

Safety

This topic can be divided into two parts—safety for the hobbyist and his home, and safety for the fishes, but both boil down to the same thing: use good heaters made by respected manufacturers, and use them in accordance with the manufacturers' instructions. Remember to observe all of the safety precautions that come into play wherever an electrical apparatus is being used near water.

There are several types of aquarium thermometers, including free-floating, standing, and those that attach to the aquarium glass.

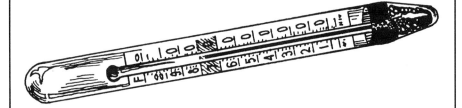

Air Pumps/Filters

Two main types of air pumps are used to supply air to filters and air stones. The first is the vibrator type which is generally smaller and less expensive than the piston type. This comes in various sizes with the smallest vibrator supplying enough air for only one filter or air stone, while the largest can service up to eighteen filters.

The air from vibrator pumps is produced under low pressure and exceptionally fine air stones will not be efficiently supplied from this source. The air supply comes from a vibrating diaphragm whose movement depends on the cycles of the alternating electrical current in the home. In the cheaper vibrators this diaphragm is made of rubber and must be replaced periodically, usually on an annual basis or when it cracks and leaks. Replacements are available at low cost and are easily installed. The larger and better vibrators use metal diaphragms and require no maintenance whatsoever. The smaller, cheaper pumps may have a sometimes annoying hum, while the better units are insulated and may be completely silent.

Piston type pumps produce air under higher pressure and generally will produce a larger volume of air than the vibrators. These depend on a standard small electric motor continuously working a small piston and cylinder and require periodic maintenance such as oiling the motor, greasing the piston washer, and occasional replacement of the drive belt. The piston pumps are usually noisier than the vibrators and are not suitable for a room where quiet is essential. Advanced hobbyists with many aquaria, or dealers and hatcheries usually require large piston pumps or regular air compressors.

Most hobbyists find that they are most successful in keeping a large aquarium clean and disease free by the use of a filter. Several types of aquarium filters are available depending on the individual aquarium situation. The outside power filter has many advantages. It is very efficient, can be run at high speeds, and is readily accessible for cleaning and for changing the filtering medium. These power filters contain water-moving motors and do not require the use of an air pump.The outside filter is also not satisfactory for a tank with fry that may get sucked into the filter intake stem.

The inside corner filter also works efficiently, and provides good aeration, but it must be connected to an air pump in order to function. It is not as easily accessible for cleaning as the outside power filter, but once out of the tank it is very easy to clean. Most of these are also poor

Inside box filters employ sound filtration principles and are easily hidden by plants or other decorations in the aquarium. Proof of their efficiency is the frequency with which they are seen in pet shop tanks which are usually heavily populated with fish. Photo by V. Serbin.

Air pumps are available with different flow rates for your particular needs. You can run just an airstone or your whole filtration system with one pump, depending on the power of the unit. Photo by V. Serbin.

Cleaning the filter medium on outside power filters is a simple procedure. Most outside power filters include floss cartridges that can be rinsed once a week and need only be replaced every several months. The filtering capacity of the outside power filter is measured in gallons per-hour. The higher the gallons per-hour ratio the stronger the filter.

for fry, although some types that are available have such narrow slits for water intake that they may be suitable for even very small babies.

Both of these types require a filtering medium that must be periodically replaced. In crowded aquaria this cleaning may have to be done on a weekly basis. The old standby in filtering material is filter floss which works well and is inexpensive. Some types have a tendency to mat, however, considerably reducing their efficiency.

Sub-sand filters are slightly raised, perforated plastic sheets that are placed on the bottom of the aquarium, then covered by the gravel. Air lift tubes are set at the rear corners. They work on a biological principle rather than by simple mechanical removal of

floating debris. These filters create a downward circulation of the aquarium water so that it passes through the gravel on the bottom of the tank to the area below the sub-sand filter and is then returned to the surface of the aquarium through the airlift tubes. In doing so, any floating debris, such as uneaten food, is deposited in the bottom gravel. The fresh constant supply of oxygenated water passing through the gravel encourages the growth of aerobic (oxygen-loving) bacteria which decompose the food under controlled conditions and convert the waste material into nitrogenous compounds (nitrites and nitrates).

If the filter is run continuously, the water will circulate constantly and the aerobic bacteria will do their job well. If the filter is turned off for more than a day or so after it has become well established and after the gravel is loaded with debris and uneaten food, the lack of fresh (oxygenated) water will kill the aerobic bacteria and a culture of anaerobic (not requiring oxygen) bacteria will rapidly develop and take over. These will also utilize the debris and food in the gravel but tend to produce toxic compounds and gases (such as hydrogen sulfide which produces the rotten egg odor noticeable in such circumstances). The water can become cloudy and foul-smelling almost overnight.

A similar situation can arise if the hobbyist finds it necessary to use antibiotics in the water; these may kill the aerobic bacteria and similarly allow the anaerobes to grow. These

A vibrator air pump provides the source of air being released from the elongated airstone shown here.

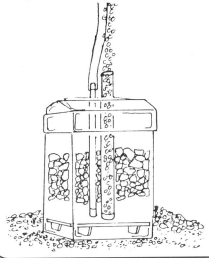

filters are also not suitable for particularly dirty fish like goldfish and larger species. Big cichlids with digging habits may also destroy the filter's efficiency by exposing it in an area free of gravel. Some hobbyists particularly interested in plants have had some difficulty with obtaining normal plant growth using these filters, possibly because of excess nitrogen compounds in the gravel. Many hobbyists introduce a sheet of plastic screen between the gravel and filter itself in order to prevent individual pieces of gravel from becoming wedged in the filter slots.

The canister filter is also quite popular. This is basically a cylindrical outside power filter that contains the filtering material. The larger ones support a certain amount of biological filtration as the water continuously flows through them thus providing the needed oxygen. Specially constructed balls or cubes that have increased surface area may also be included in the canister filter to help provide greater biological filtration. The return, as in most power filters, is forcefully sprayed into the tank to provide sufficient aeration for most tanks along with a little water movement as well.

The sponge filter is particularly well-adapted for small tanks containing fry. This type filters the water through a block of plastic foam which removes fine particles without endangering the baby fish. They are easy to clean and long lasting.

Sub-sand filters are placed below the gravel bed. They can be run by both an air pump and power head. Both the air pump and power head provide downward circulation of aquarium water through the gravel. The water is then returned to the surface of the aquarium through the plastic airlift tubes. Photo by V. Serbin.

Most box filters not only effectively clean the water in small aquaria, but provide the necessary stream of bubbles needed for sufficient oxygen for aquarium fish without the need for purchasing an additional airstone. Photo by V. Serbin.

Furnishings

The number and type of ornaments and rocks suitable for aquarium use is almost endless and is largely a matter of individual taste. It's best to purchase such things only from aquarium shops unless the hobbyist has an accurate knowledge of rocks and can choose those that are safe to keep in his aquarium water.

Petrified wood is the most frequently used standby and is quite safe as well as being attractive and available in a variety of shapes and sizes. It has an additional advantage in providing very natural-appearing surroundings with some of the pieces resembling fallen tree trunks and limbs. Castles and other artificial porcelain or plastic ornaments are safe but provide unnatural-looking surroundings for the fish.

Plants

These are the most effective ornaments and they also contribute to the maintenance of healthy conditions in the aquarium. Plants contribute by removing nitrogenous wastes (nitrates) from the water and the aquarium gravel but, contrary to popular belief, cannot be depended upon to add significant amounts of oxygen to the water. During daylight hours, plants absorb carbon dioxide from the water and do produce oxygen that returns to the water. In the dark, however, the situation is reversed and the plants then take up oxygen from the water and excrete carbon dioxide, thus nullifying their previous action.

Landscaping with plants as with ornaments and rocks is largely a matter of personal choice, but certain general rules should be followed. If a stable attractive tank requiring little pruning is desired, then rapidly growing plants such as water sprite should be avoided. Slower growing plants such as the old standby, the Amazon sword plant, are better.

Long rush-like plants, such as *Vallisneria* or *Sagittaria*, make good backgrounds in an aquarium and can provide dramatic effects when planted in clumps. These two types of plants, however, do not seem to grow well together. Bushy plants, such as *Elodea* and *Cabomba*, tend to get spindly and fall apart in aquaria, although they may do quite well in cool water ponds. They are also prone to attack by hungry fish with vegetarian tendencies. Certain fishes, such as various silver dollar species, will eat any kind of plants, and plastic plants are most practical in their tank.

Floating plants can be used to shade the aquarium from bright reflector lights and give a pleasing effect. They may also encourage particularly shy fishes, such as dwarf gouramis and some of the dwarf cichlids, to come out of hiding and to take an active part in the community tank. Some of these floating plants, such as duckweed, can be annoying and difficult to keep under control, while others, such as water sprite, are useful for shade and can be deliberately kept as an accessory supply of food for the fishes. These plants grow rapidly and can usually replenish themselves as fast as the fishes eat them.

The hobbyist must consider the amount of light available when choosing his plants. Most *Cryptocoryne* do well in relatively dim light, while *Vallisneria* or *Sagittaria* require somewhat brighter lighting. Too much light will promote the growth of algae which may form a thin layer of green growth on the aquarium glass or any surfaces in the tank. Under extreme conditions the water itself may turn a pea-soup green and the fishes will be quite difficult to see. If a growth of algae is noticed either on the glass or distributed in the water the hobbyist should cut down either the brightness of aquarium lights or their duration of burning.

Gravel

In the usual well-planted aquarium only enough gravel should be used to provide adequate rooting for the plants. Usually a layer 1-2 inches deep is sufficient to provide support for the plants' roots. An excessive amount of gravel provides a haven for uncontrolled bacterial growth and hidden food particles that may gradually rot and pollute the water.

Some hobbyists prefer to grow their plants in individual small containers, since they can be readily moved to rearrange the aquarium or if a particularly fast and wary fish must be caught. Under these conditions a layer of gravel thin enough to cover only the bottom is sufficient and will allow the fish to browse completely through it, eliminating any lost food particles.

If a sub-sand filter is used, a layer of gravel at least 1 inch thick must be used or the filter will not function efficiently.

The usual grade of aquarium gravel is satisfactory for growing most plants and for providing a bottom cover. Fine sand, such as beach sand, packs too tightly and may not allow the plants sufficient root growth, while very coarse gravel or glass or shell fragments provide too many hiding places for fallen debris. The question of natural or colored gravel is again a matter of personal taste.

Most gravel sold in aquarium shops has been pre-washed but should be rinsed again before adding it to the tank. If in doubt about the source, the gravel should be thoroughly washed in a bucket until the water runs clear.

The addition of plants, fish, driftwood, and other ornaments are what make a tank into an aquarium. The fish enjoy having nooks and crannies to investigate, but make sure that those nooks and crannies don't become repositories of decaying organic matter. Photo by B. Kahl.

A layer of one to two inches of gravel is recommended for most tanks. Adequate gravel depth is important in keeping aquarium plants well rooted and sub-sand filters working properly. Photo by V. Serbin.

Lighting

The aquarium can be placed where it receives indirect daylight but should not be placed directly in front of a window or where it will receive too much direct sunlight, or rapid algal growth will be the inevitable result. If such a location is the only one available, some protection can be given to the aquarium by the use of a paper or other background to cut down the excess outside light. The hobbyist can maintain better control of the situation if he depends on artificial lighting. The aquarium reflectors may come wired for incandescent lights which supply a good quality light for plant growth but, unfortunately, also supply excessive heat with the larger bulbs. The top layer of water may become too warm for the fishes' comfort, and water circulation should be maintained with an air stone or filter. Small aquaria will receive sufficient light from a 15- or 25-watt tubular bulb burning six to ten hours daily, depending on the type of plants utilized for decoration. Larger tanks may require two such bulbs. Most aquaria are too brightly lit, and many shy fish are frightened into darker corners.

Fluorescent reflectors are more expensive than those wired for incandescent light, but have an advantage in that they supply a cooler light without significantly affecting the water temperature. These are satisfactory for use on the aquarium with the usual daylight or warm white fluorescent bulbs and provide a quality of light adequate for plant growth. They are actually cheaper to maintain since a fluorescent bulb is more efficient than an incandescent one and gives out more light than an incandescent bulb of the same wattage.

Other types of fluorescent bulbs are available, some of which are designed specifically for promoting plant growth. They can be used in any fluorescent fixture and give out light predominantly in the red and blue wave lengths. They are not satisfactory for room lighting and provide a peculiar purple or orchid-colored tinge to their surroundings. Plant growth depends particularly on these wave lengths, however, and can be spectacular under these bulbs. Fishes with significant blue or red coloration such as neon or cardinal tetras can appear startlingly brilliant with this type of lighting. Such bulbs are usually not permitted during judging of fish shows because of the color enhancement achieved.

Aquarium reflectors can come in the form of "full hoods," which cover the entire top of the tank, or "strip" reflectors, which cover only a small part. The full hoods are more expensive, of course, but offer more protection.

pH and Hardness

The The term pH has a complicated scientific definition but for our purposes can be simply used as an indication of acidity, neutrality, or alkalinity of the aquarium water. A pH of 7 is defined as neutral while values below this are acid and above this are alkaline. Most fishes can be well-maintained in a pH range of between 6 and 7.5 while some will be happy only at even greater or lesser extremes than this. With most public water supplies it is unnecessary to alter the pH for aquarium fishes. Your local pet shop will probably be familiar with water conditions in your area and can advise you as to the usual practices.

Once in an aquarium, the water tends to become more acid as it becomes older and more and more waste materials become dissolved in it. This acidification is especially rapid and prominent in a tank with a sub-sand filter. In extreme cases the acidity can be corrected using small amounts of sodium bicarbonate added to the water, but this should be done slowly and over a period of several days if a pH change of more then 0.5 units is to be made.

Extremely alkaline water can be similarly corrected using sodium biphosphate, also available in aquarium shops. pH test kits are easy to use, but the cheap ones have relatively inaccurate printed color guides. The more expensive test kits come with glass vials containing colored solutions that can be accurately matched using the usual bromthymol blue indicator dye.

Excessively hard water may be more difficult to overcome. One solution is to dilute extremely hard tap water with either bottled distilled water or bottled spring water which is generally sold for drinking purposes. The public water supplies in most parts of the country, however, are quite suitable for aquaria. The gradual buildup of excessive hardness because of evaporation and repeated water addition can be overcome by the practice of changing 10%-20% of the aquarium water weekly. This will also help prevent the build-up of excess nitrogenous wastes. Hardness test kits as well as nitrate/nitrite test kits are available at your aquarium dealer and can provide a reasonably accurate indication of your water condition.

Some hobbyists, once they know the general quality of their water—that is whether it is hard or soft, acidic or alkaline—try to match the requirements of the fish they keep to the type of water they can provide; they find this easier to do than trying to change the composition of their water.

Fluorescent lights enhance the coloration of your tropical fish and provide the right light needed for good plant growth. Photo by V. Serbin.

Where lighting is concerned, you have to reach a happy medium: Excessive aquarium lighting could lead to the tank's becoming overgrown with algae, but enough light is necessary for the health of your desired aquatic plants. Photo by V. Serbin.

Feeding

Under natural conditions fishes are browsing almost constantly and rarely come upon a large amount of food at one time. In the aquarium they also seem happiest when given several small feedings during the day rather than one large one, part of which may lie uneaten and deteriorating. A good compromise is to feed the fish twice daily, making sure that the second feeding allows time enough for the fishes to dispose of all the food before the aquarium lights are turned off.

Dried foods are the staple diet for most aquarium fishes. An important factor to consider in choosing a dried food is the percentage of protein it contains. This will be listed on the food container along with the ingredients. The better quality commercial foods contain about 30% to 40% protein and sometimes more. The poorer quality cereal type foods may be as low as 5%. There is such a large variety of carefully formulated commercial fish foods now on the market that you'll have no trouble finding good foods at your pet shop. The hobbyist must also consider requirements of special varieties of fishes, such as mollies or scats, that require a considerable amount of vegetable material in their diet. Special preparations are available for these fishes.

Regardless of the quality of dried food used, your fishes will be healthier and grow faster if their diet also includes some live or frozen foods.

Several types of live foods are available, depending on the season and the part of the country in which the hobbyist resides. Live *Daphnia* (small freshwater crustaceans) and *Tubifex* worms may be obtained from many petshops. Live adult brine shrimp are sometimes available at pet shops, and brine shrimp eggs are almost always available. Other live foods that can be purchased or raised include earthworms, white worms, and meal worms. Live foods especially adapted for baby fishes include microworms and baby brine shrimp. Both of these may be easily raised in the home, providing a ready source of nourishment for fry at any time of the year.

Varieties of frozen foods sold include many of those previously mentioned, with *Daphnia* and brine shrimp being the most commonly available. These seem about equal in nutritional value to the live foods, and in the case of brine shrimp may be somewhat safer to use, since no living parasites can be introduced into the aquarium water with the food.

Setting Up

The beginner will find his safest course is to start with a new aquarium purchased from a reputable dealer. The all-glass bonded tanks are virtually leak proof and quite strong. A new tank will not be previously contaminated from sick fishes or miscellaneous dirt that may have fallen into it. New tanks should still be thoroughly rinsed, but no soap or detergent should be used.

Occasionally a particularly good value in a clean used tank is available. Such a tank should be rinsed thoroughly and scrubbed down inside with a strong salt solution. A thick paste of moist salt granules can be used as a gentle abrasive for more effective cleaning. An older used tank that has stood empty for some time may dry out and have a tendency to leak. The newer tanks usually are relatively safe in this respect. If in doubt, the safest course is to fill the aquarium outside the home to test for leaks before bringing it into the house. A tank should always be empty, of course, before moving it. Tanks are sturdily constructed and are strong enough to hold water on a stable base, but are not intended to be lifted or moved when filled.

Once the hobbyist is satisfied that he has a clean, non-leaking aquarium he can move it to its permanent location. This should be a standard aquarium stand or a sturdy bookcase, table, or aquarium shelf. A filled aquarium weighs approximately ten pounds per gallon of water, so a flimsy end table or TV stand is no place for a large aquarium. If the aquarium shelf is slightly flexible the tank can be given a more stable base by resting it on a slab of styrofoam 1/2 to 1 inch thick on top of the shelf. Remember also that you are dealing with water and placing an aquarium on a shelf above books or electrical equipment can have disastrous consequences.

Once the tank is in place it should be filled with washed gravel and water added to within about three inches of the top. Landscaping can then be done with plants and rocks. An additional precaution can be taken if plants are obtained from a questionable source. Your aquarium dealer can supply solutions for decontaminating plants and freeing them of any possible parasites or other undesirable organisms. After the landscaping is completed, add water to about an inch below the top edge and set up the filter and heater-thermostat units.

Let the tank stand overnight to allow chlorine and excess dissolved air to dissipate. Commercial preparations are available in aquarium shops to help dissipate the chlorine quickly. Use these as directed on the container.

Tropical fish staple foods supplemented with varieties of frozen and live foods provide optimal balanced nutrition for your fish. Photo by V. Serbin.

When a curious hobbyist approaches an aquarium most fish believe they are going to be fed. Such is the case with these fancy goldfish. Photo by V. Serbin.

Your local pet shop will probably be able to supply you with inoculation material that will initiate the development of the biological filter. A waiting period of about three or more weeks is usually necessary before the nitrogen cycle has stabilized. Your dealer may help you test the water periodically, or you can do so yourself with a simple test kit.

Most fishes purchased are placed in plastic bags that can be floated in the warm, filled tank to allow their temperatures to equalize. The fishes can then be introduced gently into the aquarium and begin to explore their new surroundings.

It is inevitable that the hobbyist will occasionally add fishes and plants to his new aquarium but he should do his best to control the impulse to do this indefinitely. Sooner or later a new addition will bring in some disease or parasite and then the hobbyist may be initiated into a more unpleasant aspect of fish keeping. This is a broad subject and cannot be adequately dealt with here. The habit of isolating newly acquired fishes in a separate tank for one week before introducing them into the community aquarium is highly recommended.

CHOOSING FISHES

Fishes for the community tank should be carefully chosen rather than randomly picking unrelated fishes of various types and colors that have nothing in common with each other. Groups of four or five fish of the same type make attractive small schools, and several species can be kept in the same tank if they are of similar size and temperament. All of the various levels in the aquarium can be utilized and still not give the tank a mood of restlessness. A group of hatchetfish can be kept for surface fish, and several small schools of neon tetras, cardinal tetras, and zebras can be kept as mid-level fishes. An algae eater such as a small *Hypostomus* can complete the population. It will more than earn its keep by keeping the aquarium glass and plants clean. The tank does not require snails which often prove to be a nuisance and, once introduced, are difficult to get rid of. A single large mystery snail is interesting but can pollute the water if it dies in a hidden corner.

The following list can be used as a guide to choosing fishes for the community tank:

Surface fishes: Hatchetfishes; pearl or gold danios.

Middle levels: Most livebearers (also in upper levels); egglaying killifishes (also in upper levels); most characins (including neon and cardinal tetras, lemon tetras, rummynose tetras, etc.); zebra danios; most barbs and rasboras; anabantoids (bubblenest builders— the larger types with larger fishes only); dwarf cichlids (also in lower levels); larger cichlids (with larger fishes only).

Bottom levels: Most catfishes; clown loaches and other loaches; mormyrids (not for beginners).

SETTING UP

Before we get into great detail describing the different types of beginner fish to pick and choose from, the importance of populating the aquarium slowly can't be emphasized enough. The most common mistake made by the novice is to purchase several fishes on the first trip to the aquarium shop. Choosing fishes at this magnitude often results in instant tank failure. The wide selection of fishes available to the hobbyist can be an overwhelming experience for the beginner. Patience is essential when carefully selecting your fishes. A gradual increase in aquarium occupants will undoubtedly pay off in the long run.

There are several beautiful beginner tropical fishes to pick and choose from. Some of the more popular varieties include tetras, livebearers, anabantoids (bubblenest builders), and small catfishes. Tetras are small active fishes that require minimal care and prefer to be kept in small schools. The neon tetra *(Paracheirodon innesi)*, and the cardinal tetra *(Paracheirodon axelrodi)*, are two popular tetra species. A collection of five or six of these fluorescent beauties provide a colorful, active aquarium as they swiftly move about the tank. The rummy nose and lemon tetras are other desirable species. Although it's virtually impossible to cater to all your fishes' ideal requirements in an community tank, a happy medium for the tetras is a clean aquarium with a neutral ph (7.0), and a water temperature between 78° and 80°. They eagerly accept dry flake food.

Livebearers are also ideal beginners' fishes that work well in the community aquarium. Not only are they easy to care for, but they will breed easily in the beginner's tank, and on occasion the newly dropped fry will frequently hide in plants or ornaments and go unnoticed. Weeks later the hobbyist is confronted with a pleasant surprise when a group of young fish suddenly appear. The most popular livebearer and one that is highly recognized worldwide is the fancy guppy *(Poecilia reticulata)*. Fancy guppies are selectively bred to exhibit wonderful color patterns and long fancy fins. The livebearers will congregate at both the middle and top layers of the aquarium.

Swordtails and platies are likely to be the beginner's next best choice in the livebearer category. They provide incredibly brightly colored strains with reds, oranges, black, and blues predominating. The male swordtails are easy to distinguish from the females with their unique sword-like tails and modified anal fins called gonopodia. Both the swords and platies make for peaceful tank inhabitants. Feeding and providing suitable water requirements can be sustained with relatively little effort.

The smaller anabantoids (bubblenest builders) will also make interesting additions to the aquarium. The betta is probably one of the most well known anabantoids. The

A school of *Corydoras adolfoi* make excellent scavengers for the community aquarium. Unlike the larger more aggressive catfish species, the corys have a pleasant personality and are easily cared for in the aquarium. Photo by Dr. H. R. Axelrod.

A brilliantly colored livebearer is the blue platy, (*Xiphophorus maculatus*). Photo by M. Gilroy.

male bettas' extravagant color and long flowing fins is what makes them such a respected and sought after species. In the community aquarium they will usually do well provided they are not mixed with feisty barbs, such as the popular tiger barb *(Capoeta tetrazona)*. Over-aggressive fin nipping fish will cause tremendous damage to the fins of slow moving bettas. The bettas common name of "Siamese Fighting fish" derives from the unfortunate outcome of two male bettas mistakenly being placed in the same tank. Two male bettas will fight intensely, usually to the death, and therefore should never be placed together. Several gourami varieties, including the blue and gold gourami, are also relatively peaceful.

The breeding behavior of the Siamese fighting fish (male shown here tending his nest) has helped to make it popular.

Another recommendation for the beginners first aquarium is to include some catfishes. Small catfishes of the genus Corydoras are excellent aquarium scavengers with delightful personalities. They will often eat any leftover food that occasionally slips to the bottom of the aquarium but should also receive their own diet to keep them in the best of health. The Corydoras cats are available in several varieties and will not grow very large in the aquarium. Several of these species can be mixed peacefully with each other, thus making them perfect bottom dwellers.

A last and final suggestion in selecting the first aquarium fishes includes the addition of a small algae eater. Since algae eaters need a large vegetarian diet, the beginner should wait a few weeks until algae has grown sufficiently in the newly established aquarium. If the algae eater is placed in a new tank that lacks sufficient algae to eat, the end result may be starvation. There are many fishes that eat algae and may be considered algae eaters. Most small algae eaters of the genus *Hypostomus* are extremely effective in cleaning algae from the aquarium glass and plants. Although algae is beneficial and an important source of food for many tropical fishes, it will often become unattractive if allowed to grow excessively.

BIBLIOGRAPHY

ALL ABOUT AQUARIUMS
By Earl Schneider
ISBN 0-86622-805-5 TFH PS-601
Contents: Selecting Your Aquarium. Light And Your Aquarium. Aeration And Filtration. Furnishing Your Aquarium. Aquarium Plant Classification. Accessory Equipment. Setting Up Your Aquarium. Types Of Aquarium Fishes.
Hard cover, 5^1/2 x 8^1/2, 128 pages
63 black and white pages, 70 color photos

Starting Your Tropical Aquarium
By Dr. Herbert R. Axelrod
ISBN 0-86622-697-4 TFH PS-840
Audience: Nobody tells it better, and here Dr. Axelrod not only tells it but also shows it in more than 250 full-color photos of fish species—step-by-step, every aspect of setting up an aquarium is covered thoroughly. A tremendous value.
Hardcover, 288 pages, 5^1/2 x 8^1/2,
Contains 256 full-color photos

Community Aquariums:
A Complete Introduction
By Dr. Herbert R. Axelrod
Softcvr CO-013S
 ISBN 0-86622-283-9
Audience: The tropical fish hobby world's most famous and most respected author here provides very sensible—and very useful—advice about which species will live together peaceably, a topic of great importance. A beautiful and valuable book.
5^1/2 x 8^1/2 , 128 pages
Contains 113 full-color photos and 35 full-color line drawings

DR. AXELROD'S MINI-ATLAS OF
FRESHWATER AQUARIUM FISHES
By Dr. Herbert R. Axelrod, Dr. Warren E. Burgess, Dr. Cliff W. Emmens, et. al
ISBN 0-8622-385-1 TFH H-1090
The entire staff of TROPICAL FISH HOBBYIST magazine, aided by Prof. C. W. Emmens, pooled their talents to make this the most complete book on aquarium fishes ever published.
The photographs—over 2200 in full color—provide the same type of exciting eye appeal and identification value that have made the full-size DR. AXELROD'S ATLAS OF FRESHWATER AQUARIUM FISHES such a tremendous winner among fishbooks and have been carefully selected to include common fishes . . . those that the world's hobbyists would encounter most frequently.
Hardcover, 5^1/2 x 8^1/2, 992 pages
Over 2200 full-color photos

SETTING UP AN AQUARIUM
A Complete Introduction
By Jim Kelly
Softcvr CO-003S ISBN 0-86622-291-X
Audience: This book contains exactly the type of information that a beginner is looking for and that even experienced hobbyists can benefit from: the types of equipment available and how to use them to best effect, which fishes and plants to choose—plus care and breeding of individual species.
5^1/2 x 8^1/2, 128 pages
Contains 52 full-color photos and 32 full-color line drawings.